Dear Parents and Teachers,

In an easy-reader format, **My Readers** introduce classic stories to children who are learning to read. Nonfiction **My Readers** tell true stories and convey fascinating facts to children who are ready to read on their own.

My Readers are available in three levels:

 Level One is for the emergent reader and features repetitive language and word clues in the illustrations.

 Level Two is for more advanced readers who still need support saying and understanding some words. Stories are longer with word clues in the illustrations.

 Level Three is for independent, fluent readers who enjoy working out occasional unfamiliar words. The stories are longer and divided into chapters.

Encourage children to select books based on interests, not reading levels. Read aloud with children, showing them how to use the illustrations for clues. With adult guidance and rereading, children will eventually read the desired book on their own.

Here are some ways you might want to use this book with children:

- Talk about the title and the cover illustrations. Encourage the child to use these to predict what the story is about.
- Discuss the interior illustrations and try to piece together a story based on the pictures. Does the child want to change or adjust his first prediction?
- After children reread a story, suggest they retell or act out a favorite part.

My Readers will not only help children become readers, they will serve as an introduction to some of the finest classic children's books available today.

—LAURA ROBB
Educator and Reading Consultant

For activities and reading tips, visit myreadersonline.com.

SQUARE
FISH

An Imprint of Macmillan Children's Publishing Group

Square Fish books may be purchased for business or promotional use.
For information on bulk purchases, please contact the Macmillan Corporate and Premium
Sales Department at (800) 221-7945 x5442 or by e-mail at specialmarkets@macmillan.com.

Library of Congress Cataloging-in-Publication Data Available

ISBN 978-1-250-05568-2 (hardcover)
1 3 5 7 9 10 8 6 4 2

ISBN 978-1-250-05569-9 (paperback)
1 3 5 7 9 10 8 6 4 2

Book design by Patrick Collins/Véronique Lefèvre Sweet

Square Fish logo designed by Filomena Tuosto

Previously published in similar form in 2012 by Henry Holt and Company, LLC, an imprint of Macmillan.
First My Readers Edition: 2015

myreadersonline.com
mackids.com

This is a Level 2 book

Lexile 500L

Kate & Pippin

An Unlikely Friendship

Martin Springett
Photographs by Isobel Springett

SQUARE
FISH

Macmillan Children's Publishing Group
New York

This is Pippin.

She is a fawn—a baby deer.

Pippin waited alone in a field
for three days.

Her mother did not come back.

This is Kate.

She is a Great Dane.

Kate was sleeping in her dog bed.

She woke up and saw a fawn next to her!

Kate's owner, Isobel,

had found Pippin

and brought her home.

Kate nuzzled little Pippin.

She gave her a lick.

Pippin snuggled up close to Kate.

Kate had never had her own puppies,
but she was a gentle dog.
Isobel knew that Kate
would take good care of Pippin.

Pippin had to learn

how to drink sheep's milk

from a baby bottle.

At first, she bit the bottle

and was frustrated.

But after two days of practice,

Pippin drank.

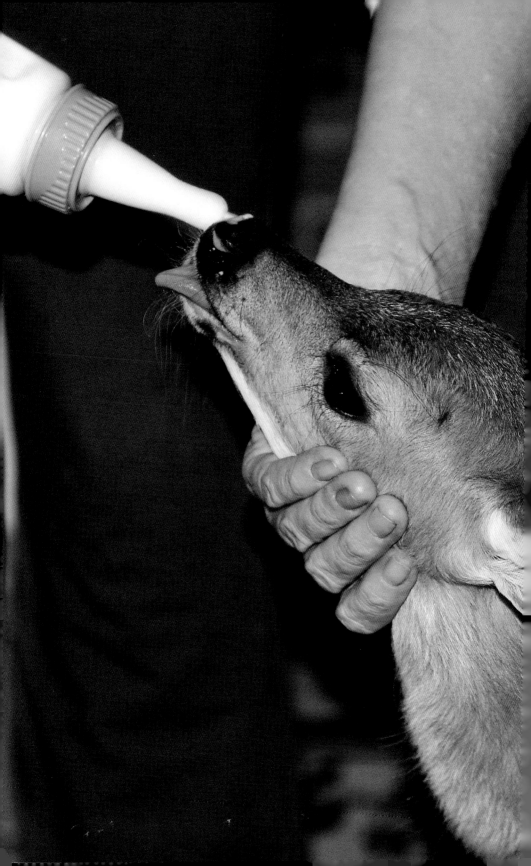

Pippin followed Kate everywhere—

just like a puppy

would follow its mother.

Pippin stayed inside for a week

so she could grow strong.

Then she followed Kate outside.

She figured out

how to climb down the stairs.

Now Kate and Pippin could play outside!

They ran around everywhere
until Kate needed a break.

One day, Pippin ran off.

Isobel called for her.

Kate waited for her to come back home.

They did not see Pippin that night.

Kate and Isobel worried

they might never see Pippin again.

The next morning,

Kate and Isobel both woke up early.

They waited.

Finally, at the edge of the trees,

there was Pippin!

Pippin came to greet Kate.

And she wanted some food.

After that, Pippin slept outside

in the forest every night.

And every day,

she came back to play with Kate

and eat snacks like bananas and bread.

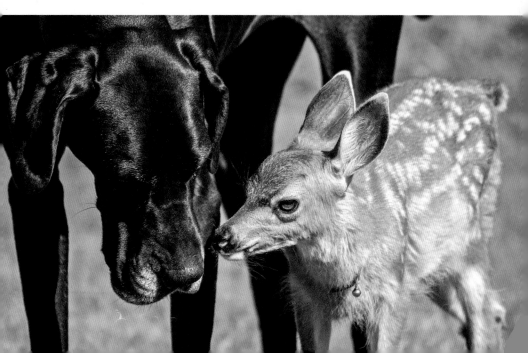

Pippin grew up quickly.
The forest was her home,
but she still came to visit.

She even became friends
with Henry the cat.

But she was still Kate's little pup.

Some time later,

Pippin brought visitors with her—

two little fawns of her own.

Now Pippin was a mother.

And Kate was a grandmother!

Pippin's babies did not come

into the house.

They did not meet Kate or Isobel.

They stayed wild.

But they were content to watch
while their mom spent time
with her family.

Kate did not go near Pippin's fawns.

Kate knew not to get too close

or she might scare them away.

Even though she was a mother now,

Pippin still liked to play with Kate!

And she still liked to give Henry a bath.

Years later,

Pippin still visits Kate almost every day.

Pippin is a wild animal

and her home is in the forest

with her babies.

But Kate and Pippin

remain the best of friends.